ISBN 978-1-330-49895-8
PIBN 10070057

For support please visit www.forgottenbooks.com

1 MONTH OF
FREE
READING

at

www.ForgottenBooks.com

By purchasing this book you are
eligible for one month membership to
ForgottenBooks.com, giving you
unlimited access to our entire
collection of over 1,000,000 titles via
our web site and mobile apps.

To claim your free month visit:

www.forgottenbooks.com/free70057

English
Français
Deutsche
Italiano
Español
Português

www.forgottenbooks.com

Mythology Photography **Fiction**
Fishing Christianity **Art** Cooking
Essays Buddhism Freemasonry
Medicine **Biology** Music **Ancient
Egypt** Evolution Carpentry Physics
Dance Geology **Mathematics** Fitness
Shakespeare **Folklore** Yoga Marketing
Confidence Immortality Biographies
Poetry **Psychology** Witchcraft
Electronics Chemistry History **Law**
Accounting **Philosophy** Anthropology
Alchemy Drama Quantum Mechanics
Atheism Sexual Health **Ancient History**
Entrepreneurship Languages Sport
Paleontology Needlework Islam
Metaphysics Investment Archaeology
Parenting Statistics Criminology
Motivational

Was Abraham Lincoln An Infidel?

THE RELIGIOUS CHARACTER OF ABRAHAM LINCOLN AS IT
APPEARS IN THE LIGHT OF HIS SPOKEN
AND WRITTEN WORD

COMPILED AND ARRANGED BY

CARL THEODOR WETTSTEIN

THE C. M. CLARK PUBLISHING COMPANY

BOSTON, MASSACHUSETTS

A Souvenir
For the Forty-fifth Anniversary of the
Death of Abraham Lincoln
April 14, 1865

Lives of great men all remind us
We can make our lives sublime,
And, departing, leave behind us
Footprints on the sands of time."
                    —*Longfellow*

PREFACE

In offering this book to the public, the writer does not claim any personal merits for its contents. It is simply a collection or compilation of the religious words of Abraham Lincoln as they were reported in the newspapers, magazines or biographies of Lincoln before, during and after the Civil War. Whenever the writer found such words, he clipped them from the papers or copied and carefully preserved them in a scrapbook. After many years he found that he had a very interesting and valuable collection.

The first words collected were the farewell address of Lincoln to the citizens of Springfield, Ill., reported in the papers on February 12, 1861, forty-nine years ago. In ordinary times this address would only have created a passing interest, and I would not have considered it worth keeping; but at that time the American people were kept in such a state of intense excitement by rumors of a threatening war, and such a dark cloud of coming unknown calamities lay over the country, that I felt as if other words of Lincoln would follow, and I collected them as soon as they were published.

Some of these utterances of Lincoln are so beautiful, so sublime, so full of faith in a Divine Ruler that they will forever remain deeply engraved in the hearts of the American people and in American history.

C. T. W.

WAS ABRAHAM LINCOLN AN INFIDEL?

IT is not the purpose at this time to depict the character of Lincoln in all its details. Should that be the purpose, no more apt words could be found than those which Lincoln himself spoke on Feb. 22, 1842, at a celebration of Washington's Birthday: "A eulogy on George Washington is expected of me. That is impossible. To give the sun more light or the name of Washington more splendor is alike impossible. No one should attempt it."

These words exactly fit Abraham Lincoln.

As at the death of men of renown, the religious or non-religious character of their lives is dwelt upon in biographies and eulogies, so, also, much has been written since Lincoln's death of his position toward religion—much that was true, much absolutely untrue. As an example of the latter, the following extract from a communication to a Chicago morning newspaper,* published many years ago, may be cited:

"From men like these (Benjamin Franklin,

Chicago Herald.

11

Thomas Jefferson, *Abraham Lincoln,* Thomas
H. Huxley, John Tyndall and Herbert Spen-
cer) the *spirit* *of infidelity* spreads down to the
lowest strata of society."

When a person of intelligence, who has read
something of Lincoln's character, sees this, he
must necessarily form the conclusion that the
writer says something of which he either has no
knowledge or purposely utters a falsehood. The
latter is the more probable. Even that apostle
of infidelity, Robert Ingersoll, was frequently
quoted as referring to Lincoln as an infidel,
and Ingersoll must have known that this was
wrong, because Lincoln's religious words have
been reported so frequently in the newspapers
that a man like Ingersoll must have read them.

We recall the following beautiful words, so
eloquently illustrating the religious character of
Lincoln:

"What appears to me to be the will of God,
that shall I do."

Had no other religious declaration been
brought down to this day than this one, it would
be sufficient to place Lincoln's religious character in a bright light. Whoever studies Lincoln's
life will know that all his after life and deeds
were indicative of an ambition to bring them into
harmony with this declaration.

It is a fact that Lincoln was not a member of
any church, but there is no doubt, had not death

Lincoln at Thirty-Nine. The Earliest Portrait
of Abraham Lincoln

claimed him so suddenly, that he would have joined a church. That he had such intentions, is confirmed by various persons. During his administration he regularly attended the Presbyterian Church of Dr. Gurney, and occasionally the church of Dr. Sutherland. Dr. Gurney says:

"Shortly before his death, Lincoln told me that he stood ready soon to affiliate with some church by confession of his faith."

In Springfield Lincoln attended the First Presbyterian Church under Dr. James Smith.

Why Lincoln should have been claimed by the Atheists as one of their faith is a mystery to me. The only motive for such an assumption can be found when, in his early youth, 1834, he wrote an essay on Thomas Payne's "Age of Reason," and Volney's "Ruins of an Empire," which he was to read before a literary society. At first he was very indignant when his friend, Sam Hill, burned the manuscript; but, later on, thanked him for it. John G. Nicolay, his private secretary, has this to say on the subject:

"Yes, there is a story, and it is probably true, that, when he was very young and very ignorant, he wrote an essay that might be called atheistical. It was after he had been reading a couple of atheistic books which made a great impression upon his mind, and the essay is supposed to have expressed his views on those books, —a sort of review of them, containing both approval and disapproval—and one of his friends burned it. He was very indignant at the time, but was afterwards glad of it."

But Lincoln's own words shall give us a correct picture of his inner life, so that the reader can form his own opinion.

JUDGE GILLESPIE AND LINCOLN

A deep impression of Lincoln's inner life, at the time between his nomination and election, has been transmitted to posterity by Judge Gillespie, who, one night at the beginning of January, stopped at Lincoln's home in Springfield. It was late before Lincoln had completed his business and the two friends sat down by the fire for a chat.

"I attempted," says Judge Gillespie, "to draw him into conversation relating to the past, hoping to divert him from the thoughts which were evidently distracting him.

" 'Yes, yes, I remember,' he would say to my references to old scenes and associations, but the old-time zest was not only lacking, but in its place was a gloom and despondency entirely foreign to Lincoln's character. . . . Suddenly he roused himself. 'Gillespie,' said he, 'I would willingly take out of my life a period in years equal to the two months which intervene between now and my inauguration, to take the oath of office now.'

" 'Why?' I asked.

" 'Because every hour adds to the difficulties I am called upon to meet, and the present administration does nothing to check the tendency toward dissolution. I, who have been called to meet this awful responsibility, am compelled to remain here, doing nothing to avert it or lessen its force when it comes to me.'

"Our talk then turned upon the possibility of avoiding a war. 'It is only possible,' said Mr. Lincoln, 'upon the consent of this government to the creation of a foreign slave government out of the present slave states. I see the duty devolving upon me. I have read, upon my knees, the story of Gethsemane, where the Son of God prayed in vain that the cup of bitterness might pass from Him. I am in the garden of Gethsemane now, and my cup of bitterness is full and overflowing.'

"I then told him that as Christ's prayer was not answered and His crucifixion had redeemed the great part of the world from paganism to Christianity, so the sacrifice demanded of him might be a great beneficence. Little did I then think how prophetic were my words to be, or what a great sacrifice he was called to make." (Ida M. Tarbell, McClure's, December, 1898.)

These words of Lincoln we can only understand if we look back upon the conditions of our country at that period.

The Cooper Institute Portrait, Taken in February, 1860

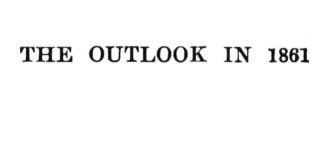

THE OUTLOOK IN 1861

"It is difficult for anybody," says Noah Brooks, "at this distance of time, and when all things are at peace throughout the republic, to realize how great was the burden placed upon Lincoln by his election to the presidency. There were two great troubles—the office-seekers and the impending war. The first of these, of course, was the smaller, but it was none the less a grievous trial. For, in addition to the strain that it brought upon his patience, it interfered very seriously with his attempt to think over the greater and far more trying questions that must soon be settled."

Ida M. Tarbell said: "Mr. Lincoln was not only obliged to sit inactive and watch this steady dissolution of the Union, but he was obliged to see what was still harder—that the administration which he was to succeed was doing nothing to check the destructionists. Indeed, all through this period, proof accumulated that members of Mr. Buchanan's cabinet had been systematically working for many months to disarm the North and equip the South. The quantity of arms sent quietly from northern arsenals (to the South) was so great that the citizens of the towns from which they went became alarmed. . . . Letters threatening him with death, sketches of gibbets, stilettos, came in every mail."

Noah Brooks concludes his article as follows: "Lincoln, at Springfield, lingering in his

home until such time as was necessary for him
to depart for Washington, beheld all these revo-
lutionary proceedings with profound anxiety.
He was powerless to lift a hand against the
traitors who were seeking the destruction of the
Federal Union, for, although he had been called
to be President of the United States, he was as
yet a private citizen. And while the loyal people
of the Republic longed and prayed for a strong
man at the helm of the national government, and
waited for the fourth of March to come and
see Abraham Lincoln in the chair of state, he
remained passive, counselling patience and
moderation to all with whom he came in contact,
and framing in his mind the pleading, expostu-
lating, and generous inaugural address that he
subsequently delivered. Jefferson Davis, on the
other hand, gave voice to the hatred and vindic-
tiveness of the slavery leaders, when, on his way
from his home to be inaugurated in Montgomery,
he said:

"'We will carry the war where it is easy
to advance, where food for the sword and the
torch awaits our armies in the densely-populated
cities.' On the one side were forbearance, mag-
nanimity, and Christian patience. On the other
side were hatred, vaporing, and threats of vio-
lence. . . . .

"Already, threats of assassination had been
whispered abroad, and it had been boasted by the

Lincoln When President-Elect

enemies of the Union that Lincoln would never reach Washington alive."

Such were the conditions in our country when Lincoln left Springfield for Washington. Can it astonish us if his heart was full of apprehension and evil forebodings for the future?

GOD'S WILL SHALL I DO

Speaking of the slaves to a member of his cabinet, he said on one occasion:

"I have not yet decided as to the proclamation of the emancipation of the slaves, but the subject has my constant consideration. I can assure you that, night and day, there is nothing that has my deeper thought. What appears to me to be God's will, that I shall do."

SHOULD BE PRINTED IN GOLDEN LETTERS

Gov. Bramlett of Kentucky, Senator Dickson and Editor A. G. Hodges came to Lincoln as bearers of a protest from the Southern states against the emancipation of the slaves. Lincoln's answer has been preserved by Hodges. Toward the end the President says:

"I add a word which was not in the verbal conversation. In telling this tale I attempt no compliment to my own sagacity. I claim not to have controlled events, but confess plainly that events have controlled me. Now, at the end of three years' struggle, the nation's condition is not what either party, or any man, devised or expected. God alone can claim it. Whither it is tending seems plain. *If God now wills the removal of a great wrong, and wills also that we of the North, as well as you of the South, shall pay fairly for our complicity in that wrong, impartial history will find therein new cause to attest and revere the justice and goodness of God."* (The Century, July, 1891.)

MEDITATION ON DIVINE WILL, SEPTEMBER 7, 1862

The will of God prevails. In great contests each party claims to act in accordance with the will of God. Both may be, and one must be, wrong. God cannot be for and against the same thing at the same time. In the present Civil War it is quite possible that God's purpose is something different from the purpose of either party; and yet the human instrumentalities, working just as they do, are of the best adaptation to effect His purpose. I am almost ready to say that this is probably true; that God wills this contest, and wills that it shall not end yet. By His mere great power on the minds of the now contestants, He could have either saved or destroyed the Union without a human contest. Yet the contest began. And, having begun, he

The Lincoln Residence at Springfield, Illinois

could give the final victory to either side any day. Yet the contest proceeds. (Nicolay and Hay.)

IN HIS FAREWELL ADDRESS AT SPRING-FIELD, FEBRUARY 11, 1861

A duty devolves upon me which is greater, perhaps, than that which has devolved upon any other man since the days of Washington. He never would have succeeded except for the aid of Divine Providence, upon which he at all times relied. I feel that I cannot succeed without the same Divine aid which sustained him, and on the same Almighty Being I place my reliance for support, and I hope you, my friends, will pray that I may receive that Divine assistance without which I cannot succeed, but with which success is certain. Again, I bid you all an affectionate farewell.

CAPTAIN MIX

Captain Mix of Lincoln's body-guard was frequently invited to breakfast with the family at the "Home" residence. "Many times," said he, "have I listened to our most eloquent preachers, but never with the same feeling of awe and reverence as when our Christian President, his arm around his son, with his deep, earnest tone, each morning, read a chapter from the Bible." (Carpenter, 261.)

LET THIS CUP PASS

Lincoln fought bitter fights with himself before he surrendered to the pressure from the abolitionists to emancipate the slaves by force of arms. He considered this act as that of a dictator. He feared it would be an abortive effort and one damaging to the loyal citizens of the South. He told a friend on one occasion that he had prayed to the Almighty to deliver him from the necessity of such a step and—using the identical words of Christ—to let the cup pass if it was at all possible. On the morning following the publication of the proclamation, he declared: "I hope to God that I have not committed an error."

LINCOLN AND NEWTON BATEMAN

Mr. Newton Bateman, Superintendent of Public Instruction for the State of Illinois, occupied a room adjoining and opening into the Executive Chamber. Frequently this door was open during Mr. Lincoln's receptions; and throughout the seven months or more of his occupation Mr. Bateman saw him nearly every day. Often when Mr. Lincoln was tired he closed his door against all intrusion, and called Mr. Bateman into his room for a quiet talk. On one of these occasions Mr. Lincoln took up a book containing a careful canvass of the city of Springfield, in which he lived, showing the candidate for whom each citizen had declared it his intention to vote in the approaching election. Mr. Lincoln's friends had, doubtless at his own request, placed the result of the canvass in his hands. This was toward the close of October, and only a few days before the election. Calling Mr. Bateman to a seat at his side, having previously locked all the doors, he said:

"Let us look over this book. I wish particularly to see how the ministers of Springfield are going to vote."

The leaves were turned, one by one, and as the names were examined Mr. Lincoln frequently asked if this one and that were not a minister, or an elder, or the member of such or such a church, and sadly expressed his surprise on receiving an affirmative answer. In that manner they went through the book, and then he closed it and sat silently and for some minutes regarded a memorandum in pencil which lay before him. At length he turned to Mr. Bateman, with a face full of sadness, and said:

"Here are twenty-three ministers, of different denominations, and all of them are against me but three, and here are a great many prominent members of the churches, a very large majority of whom are against me. Mr. Bateman, I am not a Christian—God knows I would be one—but I have carefully read the Bible, and I do not so understand this book;" and he drew from his bosom a pocket New Testament. "These men well know," he continued, "that I am for freedom in the territories, freedom everywhere as far as the Constitution and laws will permit, and that my opponents are for slavery. They know this, and yet, with this book in their hands, in the light of which human bondage cannot live a moment, they are going to vote against me. I do not understand it at all."

Here Mr. Lincoln paused—paused for long minutes, his features surcharged with emotion. Then he rose and walked up and down the room in the effort to retain or regain his self-possession. Stopping at last, he said, with a trembling voice and his cheeks wet with tears:

"I know there is a God, and that He hates injustice and slavery. I see the storm coming, and

I know that His hand is in it. If He has a place and work for me—and I think He has—I believe I am ready. I am nothing, but truth is everything. I know I am right because I know that liberty is right, for Christ teaches it, *and Christ is God.* I have told them that a house divided against itself cannot stand, and Christ and reason say the same; and they will find it so. Douglas doesn't care whether slavery is voted up or down, but God cares, and humanity cares, and I care; and with God's help I shall not fail. I may not see the end; but it will come, and I shall be vindicated; and these men will find that they have not read their Bibles aright."

Much of this was uttered as if he were speaking to himself, and with a sad and earnest solemnity of manner impossible to be described. After a pause, he resumed:

"Doesn't it appear strange that men can ignore the moral aspects of this contest? A revelation could not make it plainer to me that slavery or the government must be destroyed. The future would be something awful, as I look at it, but for this rock on which I stand" (alluding to the Testament which he still held in his hand), "especially with the knowledge of how these ministers are going to vote. It seems as if God had borne with this thing (slavery) until the very teachers of religion have come to defend it from the Bible, and to claim for it a divine character and sanction; and now the cup of iniquity is full, and the vials of wrath will be poured out."

His last reference was to certain prominent clergymen in the South, Drs. Ross and Palmer among the number; and he went on to comment on the atrociousness and essential blasphemy of their attempts to defend American slavery from the Bible. After this the conversation was continned for a long time. Everything he said was of a peculiarly deep, tender and religious tone, and all was tinged with a touching melancholy. He repeatedly referred to his conviction that the day of wrath was at hand, and that he was to be an actor in the terrible struggle which would issue in the overthrow of slavery, though he might not live to see the end. He repeated many passages of the Bible, and seemed specially impressed with the solemn grandeur of portions of Revelations, describing the wrath of Almighty God. In the course of the conversation he dwelt much upon the necessity of faith in the Christian's God as an element of successful statesmanship, especially in times like those which were upon him, and said that it gave that calmness and tranquillity of mind, that assurance of ultimate success, which made a man firm and immovable amid the wildest excitements. After further reference to a belief in Divine Providence, and the fact of God in history, the conver-

Lincoln in His Prime

sation turned upon prayer. He freely stated his belief in the duty, privilege and efficacy of prayer, and intimated, in unmistakable terms, that he had sought in that way the Divine guidance and favor.

The effect of this conversation upon the mind of Mr. Bateman, a Christian gentleman whom Mr. Lincoln profoundly respected, was to convince him that Mr. Lincoln had, in his quiet way, found a path to the Christian standpoint— that he had found God, and rested on the eternal truth of God. As the two men were about to separate, Mr. Bateman remarked: "I have not supposed that you were accustomed to think so much upon this class of subjects. Certainly your friends generally are ignorant of the sentiments you have expressed to me." He replied quickly: "I know they are. I am obliged to appear indifferent to them; but I think more on these subjects than upon all others, and I have done so for years, and I am willing that *you* should know it."

This remarkable conversation furnishes a golden link in the chain of Mr. Lincoln's history. It flashes a strong light upon the path he had already trod, and illuminates every page of his subsequent record. Men have wondered at his abounding charity, his love of mankind, his equanimity under the most distressing circumstances, his patience under insult and misrepresentation, his delicate consideration of the feelings of the humble, his apparent incapacity of resentment, his love of justice, his transparent simplicity, his truthfulness, his good will toward his enemies, his beautiful and unshaken faith in the triumph of the right.   There was undoubtedly something in his natural constitution that favored the development of these qualities; but those best acquainted with human nature will hardly attribute the combination of excellencies which were exhibited in his character and life to the unaided forces of his constitution.   The man who carried what he called "this rock" in his bosom, who prayed, who thought more on religious subjects than of all others, who had an undying faith in the providence of God, drew his life from the highest fountains.

It was one of the peculiarities of Mr. Lincoln to hide these religious experiences from the eyes of the world.   In the same State House where this conversation occurred, there were men who imagined—who really believed—who freely said—that Mr. Lincoln had probably revealed himself with less restraint to them than to others: —men who thought they knew him as they knew their bosom companions—who had never in their whole lives heard from his lips one word of all these religious convictions and experiences. They did not regard him as a religious man. They had never seen anything but the active lawyer, the keen politician, the jovial, fun-loving companion, in Mr. Lincoln. All this department of his life he had kept carefully hidden from them. Why he should say that he was obliged to appear differently to others does not appear; but the fact is a matter of history that he never exposed his own religious life to those who had no sympathy with it. It is doubtful whether the clergymen of Springfield knew anything of these experiences. Very few of them were in political sympathy with him; and it is evident that he could open his heart to no one except under the most favorable circumstances. The well-spring from which gushed up so grand and good a life was kept carefully covered from the eyes of the world. Its possessor looked into it often, but the careless or curious crowd were never favored with the vision. There was much in his conduct that was simply a cover to these thoughts—an attempt to conceal them. It is more than probable that, on separating from Mr. Bateman on this occasion, he met some old friend, and, leaping at a single bound from his tearful melancholy and his sublime religious passion, he told him some story, or indulged in some jest, that filled his own heart with mirthfulness, and awoke convulsions of laughter in him who heard it. (Holland, 236.)

Mr. Carpenter, referring to this conversation with Bateman, said: "I myself had an impression as though I stood before one of the ancient prophets when Lincoln spoke of the situation and the future of the United States."

From the Collection of Robert Coster

THE DEATH OF WILLIE LINCOLN

Lincoln's religious character apparently was clarified and strengthened, not only by the death of his son, Willie, but particularly by reason of the grave responsibilities resting upon his shoulders and the portentous occurrences that played before his eyes and took place under his own direction. Lincoln's deep, earnest, religious awakening apparently, however, dates from the death of his son, William Wallace, who died, twelve years of age, February 20, 1862.

Mr. Carpenter was busy in the White House painting the historical picture, "The Emancipation Proclamation." During this time he became most intimately acquainted with Lincoln. In his book, "The Inner Life of Abraham Lincoln." he says:

"William Wallace Lincoln, I never knew. He died Thursday, February 20th, 1862, nearly two years before my intercourse with the President commenced. He had just entered upon his twelfth year, and has been described to me as of an unusually serious and thoughtful disposition. His death was the most crushing affliction Mr. Lincoln had ever been called upon to pass through.

"After the funeral, the President resumed his official duties, but mechanically, and with a terrible weight at his heart. The following Thursday he gave way to his feelings, and shut himself from all society. The second Thursday it was the same; he would see no one, and seemed a prey to the deepest melancholy. About this time the Rev. Francis Vinton, of Trinity Church, New York, had occasion to spend a few days in Washington. As an acquaintance of Mrs. Lincoln and her sister, Mrs. Edwards, of Springfield, he was requested by them to come up and see the President. The setting apart of Thursday for the indulgence of his grief had gone on for several weeks, and Mrs. Lincoln began to be seriously alarmed for the health of her husband, of which Dr. Vinton was apprised. Mr. Lincoln received him in the parlor, and an opportunity was soon embraced by the clergyman to chide him for showing so rebellious a disposition to the decrees of Providence. He told him plainly that the indulgence of such feelings, though natural, was sinful. It was unworthy one who believed in the Christian religion. He had duties to the living, greater than those of any other man, as the chosen father and leader of the people, and he was unfitting himself for his responsibilities by thus giving way to his grief. To mourn the departed as lost is a relic of heathenism—not Christianity.

" 'Your son,' said Dr. Vinton, 'is alive, in Paradise. Do you remember that passage in the Gospels: "God is not the God of the dead but of the living, for all live unto Him"?'

"The President had listened as one in a stupor

until his ear caught the words, 'Your son is alive.' Starting from the sofa, he exclaimed, 'Alive! alive! Surely you mock me.'

" 'No, sir; believe me,' replied Dr. Vinton; 'it is a most comforting doctrine of the church, founded upon the words of Christ Himself.'

"Mr. Lincoln looked at him a moment, and then, stepping forward, he threw his arm around the clergyman's neck, and laying his head upon his breast, sobbed aloud. 'Alive? alive?' he repeated.

" 'My dear sir,' said Dr. Vinton, greatly moved, as he twined his own arm around the weeping father, 'believe this, for it is God's most precious truth. "Seek not your son among the dead; he is not there; he lives to-day in Paradise!" Think of the full import of the words I have quoted. The Sadducees, when they questioned Jesus, had no other conception than that Abraham, Isaac, and Jacob were dead and buried. Mark the reply: Now that the dead are raised, even Moses showed at the bush when he called the Lord the God of Abraham, the God of Isaac, and the God of Jacob. For He is not the God of the dead, but of the living, for all live unto Him. Did not the aged patriarch mourn his sons as dead?— "Joseph is not, and Simeon is not, and ye will take Benjamin also." But Joseph and Simeon were both living, though he believed it not. Indeed, Joseph being taken from him, was the eventual

means of the preservation of the whole family.
And so God has called your son into His upper
kingdom—a kingdom and an existence as real,
more real, than your own. It may be that he,
too, like Joseph, has gone, in God's good providence, to be the salvation of his father's household. It is a part of the Lord's plan for the
ultimate happiness of you and yours. Doubt it
not. I have a sermon,' continued Dr. Vinton,
'upon this subject which I think might interest
you.'

"Mr. Lincoln begged him to send it at an
early day—thanking him repeatedly for his cheer-
ing and hopeful words. The sermon was sent,
and read over and over by the President, who
caused a copy to be made for his own private
use before it was returned. Through a member
of the family, I have been informed that Mr.
Lincoln's views in relation to spiritual things
seemed changed from that hour. Certain it is,
that thenceforth he ceased the observance of the
day of the week upon which his son died, and
gradually resumed his accustomed cheerfulness.'"

On this subject Holland says, p. 434:

"In February, 1862, Mr. Lincoln was visited
by severe affliction in the death of his beautiful
son, Willie, and the extreme sickness of Thomas,
familiarly called 'Tad.' This was a new burden; and the visitation which, in his firm faith
in Providence, he regarded as providential, was

Lincoln and Tad

also inexplicable. Why should he, with so many burdens upon him, and with such necessity for solace in his home and his affections, be brought into so tender a trial? It was to him a trial of faith, indeed. A Christian lady of Massachusetts, who was officiating as nurse in one of the hospitals, came in to attend the sick children. She reports that Mr. Lincoln watched with her about the bedside of the sick ones, and that he often walked the room, saying sadly:

" 'This is the hardest trial of my life; why is it? Why is it?'

"In the course of conversations with her, he questioned her concerning her situation. She told him she was a widow, and that her husband and two children were in Heaven; and added that she saw the hand of God in it all, and that she had never loved Him so much before as she had since her affliction.

" 'How is that brought about?' inquired Mr. Lincoln.

" 'Simply by trusting in God, and feeling that He does all things well,' she replied.

" 'Did you submit fully under the first loss?' he asked.

" 'No,' she answered, 'not wholly; but, as blow came upon blow, and all were taken, I could and did submit, and was very happy.'

"He responded: 'I am glad to hear you say that. Your experience will help me to bear my afflictions.'

"On being assured that many Christians were praying for him on the morning of the funeral, he wiped away the tears that sprang in his eyes, and said: 'I am glad to hear that. I want them to pray for me. I need their prayers.' As he was going out to the burial, the good lady expressed her sympathy with him. He thanked her gently, and said: 'I will try to go to God with my sorrows.' A few days afterwards, she asked him if he could trust God. He replied: 'I think I can, and I will try. I wish I had that child-like faith you speak of, and I trust He will give it to me.' And then he spoke of his mother, whom so many years before he had committed to the dust among the wilds of Indiana. In this hour of his great trial, the memory of her who had held him upon her bosom, and soothed his childish griefs, came back to him with tenderest recollections.

" 'I remember her prayers,' said he, 'and they have always followed me. They have clung to me all my life.'

"This lady was with the President on subsequent occasions. After the second defeat at Bull Run, he appeared very much distressed about the number of killed and wounded, and said:

" 'I have done the best I could. I have asked God to guide me, and now I must leave the event with Him.' On another occasion, having been made acquainted with the fact that a great battle was in progress, at a distant but important point, he came into the room, where the lady was engaged in nursing a member of the family, looking worn and haggard, and saying that he was so anxious that he could eat nothing. The possibility of defeat depressed him greatly; but the lady told him he must trust, and he could at least pray.

" 'Yes,' said he, and taking up a Bible, he started for his room. Could all the people of the nation have overheard the earnest petition that went up from that inner chamber, as it reached the ears of the nurse, they would have fallen upon their knees with tearful and reverential sympathy. At one o'clock in the afternoon, a telegram reached him announcing a Union victory; and then he came directly to the room, his face beaming with joy, saying:

" 'Good news! Good news! The victory is ours, and God is good.'

" 'Nothing like prayer,' suggested the pious lady, who traced a direct connection between the event and the prayer which preceded it.

" 'Yes there is,' he replied,— 'praise:—prayer and praise.'

"The good lady who communicates these incidents closes them with the words: 'I do believe he was a true Christian, though he had very little confidence in himself.' "

LINCOLN AND GENERAL SICKLES

James F. Rusling relates in the New York Tribune the following impressive utterance, which was made in his hearing during Mr. Lincoln's visit to General Sickles, who had been wounded at the battle of Gettysburg a day or two before. It was Sunday morning, July 5, 1863. Mr. Lincoln greeted Sickles right cordially and tenderly, though cheerfully, and it was easy to see that they held each other in high esteem. Greetings over, Mr. Lincoln dropped into a chair and, crossing his prodigious legs, soon fell to questioning Sickles as to all the phases of the combat at Gettysburg. When Mr. Lincoln's inquiries ended, General Sickles resumed the conversation substantially as follows:

"Well, Mr. President, I beg pardon, but what do you think about Gettysburg? What was your opinion of things while we were campaigning and fighting up there in Pennsylvania?"

"Oh," replied Mr. Lincoln, "I didn't think much about it. I was not much concerned about you!"

"You were not?" rejoined Mr. Sickles, amazed. "Why, we heard that you Washington folks were a good deal excited, and you certainly had good cause to be, for it was 'nip and tuck' with us up there a good deal of the time!"

"Yes, I know that, and I suppose some of us were a little 'rattled.' Indeed, some of the Cabinet talked of Washington's being captured, and ordered a gunboat or two here, and even went so far as to send some Government archives aboard, and wanted me to go, too, but I refused. Stanton and Welles, I believe, were both 'stampeded' somewhat, and Seward, I reckon, too. But I said, 'No, gentlemen, we are all right, and are going to win at Gettysburg;' and we did, right handsomely. No, General Sickles, I had no fears of Gettysburg."

"Why not, Mr. President? How was that? Pretty much everybody down here, we heard, was more or less panicky."

"Yes, I expect so, and a good many more than will own up now. But actually, General Sickles, I had no fears of Gettysburg, and if you really want to know I will tell you why. Of course, I don't want you and Colonel Rusling to say anything about this—at least, not now. People might laugh if it got out, you know. But the fact is, in the stress and pitch of the campaign there, I went to my room, and got down on my knees and prayed Almighty God for victory at Gettysburg. I told Him that this was His country, and the war was His war, but that we really couldn't stand another Fredericksburg or Chancellorsville. And then and there I made a solemn vow with my Maker that if He would stand by you boys at Gettysburg, I would stand by Him. And He did; and I will! And, after this, I don't know how it was, and it is not for me

"The Council of War"—A War-Time Print

to explain, but somehow or other a sweet comfort crept into my soul that God Almighty had taken the whole thing into His own hands, and we were bound to win at Gettysburg! No, General Sickles, I had no fears of Gettysburg; and that is the reason why!"

Mr. Lincoln said all this with great solemnity and impressiveness, almost as Moses might have spoken when he first came down from Sinai; and when he had concluded, there was a pause in the talk that nobody seemed disposed to break. All were busy with their thoughts, and the President especially appeared to be communing with the Infinite One again. The first to speak was General Sickles, who presently resumed as follows:

"Well, Mr. President, what are you thinking about Vicksburg, nowadays?"

"Oh," answered Mr. Lincoln, very gravely. "I don't quite know. Grant is still pegging away down there, and making some headway, I believe. As we used to say out in Illinois, I think 'he will make a spoon or spoil a horn' before he gets through."

"So, then, you have no fears about Vicksburg, either, Mr. President?" asked General Sickles.

"Well, no; I can't say that I have," replied Mr. Lincoln, very soberly. "The fact is—but don't say anything about this either just now—I have been praying to Almighty God for Vicksburg, also." Of course Mr. Lincoln did not then know that Vicksburg had already fallen on July 4th.

THE LADY OF THE CHRISTIAN COMMISSION

The Rev. Mr. Willets, of Brooklyn, gave Carpenter an account of a conversation with Mr. Lincoln on the part of a lady of his acquaintance, connected with the "Christian Commission," who in the prosecution of her duties had several interviews with him. The President, it seemed, had been much impressed with the devotion and earnestness of purpose manifested by the lady, and on one occasion, after she had discharged the object of her visit, he said to her:

"Mrs. ———, I have formed a high opinion of your Christian character, and now, as we are alone, I have a mind to ask you to give me, in brief, your idea of what constitutes a true religious experience."

The lady replied at some length, stating that, in her judgment, it consisted of a conviction of one's own sinfulness and weakness, and personal need of a Savior for strength and support; that views of mere doctrine might and would differ, but when one was really brought to feel his need of Divine help, and to seek the aid of the Holy Spirit for strength and guidance, it was satisfactory evidence of his having been born again. This was the substance of her reply. When she had concluded, Mr. Lincoln was very thoughtful for a few moments. At length he said, very earnestly:

"If what you have told me is really a correct view of this great subject, I think I can say with sincerity, that I hope I am a Christian. I had lived," he continued, "until my boy, Willie, died, without realizing fully these things. That blow overwhelmed me. It showed me my weakness as I had never felt it before, and if I can take what you have stated as a test, I think I can safely say that I know something of the change of which you speak; and I will further add, that it has been my intention for some time, at a suitable opportunity, to make a public confession of my faith."

This latter remark means, as is well known, the joining of a church.

Lincoln in 1860

LINCOLN AND THE OLD QUAKERESS

At a dinner party in Washington, composed mainly of opponents of the war and the administration, Mr. Lincoln's course and policy were, as usual with this class, the subjects of vehement denunciation. This had gone on for some time, when one of the company, who had taken no part in the discussion, asked the privilege of saying a few words.

"Gentlemen," said he, "you may talk as you please about Mr. Lincoln's capacity; I don't believe him to be the ablest statesman in America, by any means, and I voted against him on both occasions of his candidacy. But I happened to see, or, rather, to hear something, the other day, that convinced me that, however deficient he may be in the head, he is all right in the heart. I was up at the White House, having called to see the President on business. I was shown into the office of his private secretary, and told that Mr. Lincoln was busy just then, but would be disengaged in a short time. While waiting, I heard a very earnest prayer being uttered in a loud, female voice in the adjoining room. I inquired what it meant, and was told that an old Quaker lady, a friend of the President's, had called that afternoon and taken tea at the White House, and that she was then praying with Mr. Lincoln. After the lapse of a few minutes the prayer ceased, and the President, accompanied by a Quakeress not less than eighty years old, entered the room where I was sitting. I made up my mind then, gentlemen, that Mr. Lincoln was not a bad man; and I don't think it will be easy to efface the impression that the scene I witnessed and the voice I heard made on my mind."

COLONEL LOOMIS

An illustration of Mr. Lincoln's interest in the efforts of religious men is found in his treatment of a case brought before him by the Rev. Mr. Duryea. Colonel Loomis, commandant at Fort Columbus, on Governor's Island, was to be retired because he had passed the legal limit of age for active service. His religious influence was so powerful that the Chaplain of the post appealed to Mr. Duryea to use his influence for the good officer's retention in the service. Accordingly, appeal was made to the President for that object, purely on religious grounds.

"What does Mr. Duryea know of military matters?" inquired Mr. Lincoln, with a smile, of the bearer of the petition.

"Nothing," replied the gentleman; "and he makes no request on military considerations. The record of Colonel Loomis for fifty years, in the War Department, will furnish these. He asks simply to retain the influence of a man whose Christian character is pure and consistent, who sustains religious exercises at the fort, leads

Lincoln in His Circuit Riding Days

1851, during a severe illness of his father, he writes:

"I earnestly hope that father will recover, but, above all things, tell him to confide in our benevolent and kind Creator, who will not forsake him in any tribulation. He will not forsake the dying who put their trust in Him. Tell him that if it is decreed that he shall leave us, he will have a glorious reunion with the loved ones gone before, and where we others, left behind, hope soon to be reunited with him."

TRUE RELIGION IN POLITICS

In the Legislature, where discreditable means were employed to pass a bill: "You may burn my body to ashes and scatter them to the four winds of Heaven; you may drag my soul down to the regions of darkness and despair, to be tormented forever; *but you will not get me to support a measure which I believe to be wrong.*"

"Nearly eighty years ago we declared that all men are created equal," he said in 1854, "but now we declare that for certain men it is a divine right of self-government to make slaves of other men. These principles cannot exist together. They oppose each other like God and Mammon."

In the debate with Douglas at Charleston:

"I do not want to be understood as believing

that it (the agitation for the abolition of slavery)
will be ended in a day, a year, or in two years.
I do not believe that the abolition of slavery can
be brought about peaceably in a hundred years,
but that it will be accomplished in God's own
good time in the best way for both races, of that
I have not the least doubt."

DRINKS ADAM'S ALE FROM WELL

Lincoln, as is well known, never drank alco-
holic liquors, although he was no fanatic on this
question. When the committee, which notified
him of his candidacy for the presidency, were
seated, Lincoln ordered the servant girl to bring
some refreshments. A jug of water and glasses
were placed upon the table, Lincoln saying:

"Gentlemen, let us drink to our mutual good
health in this most wholesome drink which God
has given us. It is the only drink which I permit
in my family and in all conscience let me not depart from this custom on this occasion. It is
the purest Adam's ale, fresh from the well."

AT ALBANY, NEW YORK

In a speech at Albany, N. Y., he said:
"I still have confidence that the Almighty
Ruler of the universe, through the instrumen-
tality of this great and intelligent people, can

and will bring us through this difficulty as He has heretofore brought us through all preceding difficulties of the country. Relying upon this, and again thanking you, as I forever shall, in my heart, for this generous reception you have given me, I bid you farewell."

AT TRENTON, NEW JERSEY

"I am exceedingly anxious that this Union, the Constitution, and the liberties of the people, shall be perpetuated in accordance with the original idea for which that struggle was made, and I shall be most happy indeed if I shall be an humble instrument in the hands of the Almighty, and of this, His almost chosen people, for perpetuating the object of that great struggle."

TO THE LEGISLATURE OF OHIO, COLUMBUS, FEBRUARY 13, 1861

"Very great responsibility rests upon me in the position to which the votes of the American people have called me. I am deeply sensible of that weighty responsibility. I cannot but know what you all know, that without a name, perhaps without a reason why I should have a name, there has fallen upon me a task such as did not rest even upon the Father of his Country; and so feeling, I can turn and look for that support without which it will be impossible for me to perform that great task. I turn, then, and look to the American people, and to that God who has never forsaken them."

IN PHILADELPHIA, FEBRUARY 22, 1861

"My friends, this is wholly an unprepared speech. I did not expect to be called on to say a word when I came here. I supposed I was merely to do something toward raising a flag. I may, therefore, have said something indiscreet." (Cries of "No, no.") "But I have said nothing but what I am willing to live by, and, if it be the pleasure of Almighty God, to die by."

TO MRS. BIXBY

For many days after the result of his second election was known, Mr. Lincoln was burdened with congratulations; and yet, amid these disturbances, and the cares of office, which were onerous in the extreme, he found time to write the following letter:

"Executive Mansion, Washington, Nov. 21, 1864.

"Dear Madam:—I have been shown, in the files of the War Department, a statement by the Adjutant-General of Massachusetts, that you are

Lincoln in 1860

the mother of five sons who have died gloriously on the field of battle. I feel how weak and fruitless must be any words of mine which should attempt to beguile you from the grief of a loss so overwhelming. But I cannot refrain from tendering to you the consolation that may be found in the thanks of the republic they died to save. I pray that our Heavenly Father may assuage the anguish of your bereavement, and leave you only the cherished memory of the loved and lost, and the solemn pride that must be yours to have laid so costly a sacrifice upon the altar of freedom."

The Hon. James Bryce, English Ambassador to Washington, said of this letter: "It deals with a theme on which hundreds of letters are written daily. But I do not know where the nobility of self-sacrifice for a great cause, and of the consolation which the thought of a sacrifice so made should bring, is set forth with such simple and pathetic beauty."

CHRISTIAN SABBATH

Requested to preside over a meeting of the Christian Commission Feb. 22, 1863, in Washington, Lincoln said:

"That Washington's birthday and the Christian Sunday fall this time on the same day, indicating the highest interests of this life and that beyond, is most significant for the proposed meeting."

LINCOLN AND DR. SUNDERLAND

Byron Sunderland, Chaplain of the Senate, and others were afraid that Lincoln would not issue his emancipation proclamation. On the Sunday before January 1, 1863, Dr. Sunderland preached on this subject, and F. S. Robbins, a friend of Lincoln, requested him to go to Lincoln and try to persuade him to issue the proclamation. In this conversation, Lincoln said:

"Were it left to me and you, doctor, there would have been no war; yes, there would not have been any cause for war. But it was not left to us. God permitted men to make slaves of their fellowmen. He also permitted this war. He has staged a peculiar drama before His eye. We on our side appeal to Him for victory, because we believe we are right, but those on the other side likewise appeal to Him for victory, because they believe they are right. What must He think of us? And what will be the result?"

"And then," continues Sunderland, "Lincoln discussed the situation with us in such clear, convincing language as to strengthen and convince me so that since that hour I have placed fullest confidence in him. His words appealed to me like those of one of the old Prophets."

MRS. LINCOLN

Mrs. Lincoln said: "One day, after breakfast, soon after he had finished his first inaugural ad-

A Rare Photograph of Mrs Lincoln

dress, he ordered the whole family out of the room. I was in the adjoining room and saw how he knelt down, and then I heard him pray to God for strength and wisdom in the fulfillment of his duties."

BISHOP SIMPSON

"One day, during the darkest hours of the war," said Bishop Simpson to Chaplain C. E. McCabe, "I went to Lincoln. We had a long talk about the situation. When I was ready to go, Lincoln locked the door, and said: 'Bishop, I feel the need of prayer more than ever before; please, do pray for me.' And we knelt down in an earnest prayer, and the President responded from the bottom of his heart."

GENERAL O. O. HOWARD

General O. O. Howard said at the consecration of Chickamauga Park:

"It is said that Lincoln, during the battle of Gettysburg, was in a worse state of excitement and mental anguish than if he had been present personally in the battle, and that this brought on a spiritual change in his soul, which, later on, became a deep submission and resignation to the will of God."

PRAYER

During one of the great battles near Washington, Lincoln was seen going into his room with his Bible. Then he was heard to pray aloud, so sincere, so earnest, so full of emotion, as only a true Christian can pray.

AFTER THE BATTLE OF BULL RUN

After the second battle of Bull Run, Lincoln was deeply depressed because of the heavy losses of the Union army. "I have done as well as I could," said he at the time to a woman friend. "I prayed to God to direct me the right way and now I must leave the consequences to Him alone."

LINCOLN'S MOTHER

His mother laid the foundation for Lincoln's religious character. After he became President he said, speaking of his mother:

"I recall her prayers that she was wont to offer on Sundays with her children after she had read to them stories from the Bible. They have followed me everywhere and have remained with me all through life."

THE CHURCH HE WANTS TO JOIN

"On an occasion I shall never forget," says the Hon. H. C. Deming, of Connecticut, "the conversation turned upon religious subjects, and Mr. Lincoln made this impressive remark: 'I have never united myself to any church, because I have found difficulty in giving my assent, without mental reservation, to the long, complicated statements of Christian doctrine which characterize their Articles of Belief and Confessions of Faith. When any church will inscribe over its altar, as its sole qualification for membership,' he continued, 'the Savior's condensed statement of the substance of both Law and Gospel, "Thou shalt love the Lord thy God with all thy heart, and with all thy soul, and with all thy mind, and thy neighbor as thyself," that church will I join with all my heart and all my soul.' "

WILL BE A BETTER MAN

At another time he said, cheerfully: "I am very sure that if I do not go away from here a wiser man, I shall go away a better man, for having learned here what a very poor sort of a man I am."

Afterwards, referring to what he called "a change of heart," he said, he did not remember any precise time when he passed through any special change of purpose, or of heart; but he would say, that his own election to office, and the crisis immediately following, influentially determined him in what he called "a process of crystallization," then going on in his mind. Reticent as he was, and shy of discoursing much on his own mental exercises, these few utterances now have a value with those who knew him, which his dying words would scarcely have possessed. (Brooks.)

FIRM BELIEF IN OVER-RULING PROVIDENCE

On another occasion, when a number of the members of the commission were holding an interview with the President, Rev. J. T. Duryea of New York referred to the trust that they were encouraged to repose in the Providence of God, and to the fact that appeal was so constantly made to it in the prayers of Christian people that even children were taught to pray for the President in their simple morning and evening petitions.

"If it were not for my firm belief in an over-ruling Providence," responded Mr. Lincoln, "it would be difficult for me, in the midst of such complications of affairs, to keep my reason on its seat. But I am confident that the Almighty has His plans, and will work them out; and, whether we see it or not, they will be the wisest and best for us. I have always taken counsel of Him, and referred to Him my plans, and have never adopted a course of proceeding without being assured, as far as I could be, of His approbation. To be sure, He has not conformed to my desires, or else we should have been out of our trouble long ago. On the other hand, His will does not seem to agree with the wish of our enemy over there" (pointing across the Potomac). "He stands the Judge between us, and we ought to be willing to accept His decisions. We have

A Rare Lincoln Photograph

reason to anticipate that it will be favorable to us, for our cause is right." It was during this interview that the fact was privately communicated to a member of the commission, that Mr. Lincoln was in the habit of spending an early hour each day in prayer.

When, in the eventful days after the election of 1860, the Southern States were rapidly seceding, and the fate of the Union seemed so dark and ominous, it was a Springfield citizen and neighbor of Lincoln, William H. Herndon, who, in answer to a New England correspondent anxiously inquiring if, in his opinion, the Western circuit-court lawyer who had just been elected to the Presidency would be big and brave enough to deal with the great and tremendous problems that awaited him, said:

"You need have no fear on that score. You and I must keep the people right; God will keep Abraham Lincoln right."

TO DELEGATIONS

TO THE BAPTIST MINISTERS, MAY 30, 1864

"In response to the preamble and resolutions of
the American Baptist Home Mission Society,
which you did me the honor to present, I can
only thank you for thus adding to the effective
and almost unanimous support which the Christian communities are so zealously giving to the
country and to liberty.   Indeed, it is difficult
to conceive how it could be otherwise with any
one professing Christianity, or even having ordinary perceptions of right and wrong.   To read
in the Bible, as the word of God Himself, that 'In
the sweat of thy face shalt thou eat bread,' and
to preach therefrom that, 'In the sweat of other
men's faces shalt thou eat bread,' to my mind
can scarcely be reconciled with honest sincerity.
When brought to my final reckoning, may I have
to answer for robbing no man of his goods; yet
more tolerable even this, than robbing one of
himself and all that was his.   When, a year or
two ago, those professedly holy men of the South
met in the semblance of prayer and devotion, and,
in the name of Him who said, 'As ye would all
men should do unto you, do ye even so unto
them,' appealed to the Christian world to aid
them in doing to a whole race of men as they
would have no man do unto themselves, to my
thinking they contemned and insulted God and
His church far more than did Satan when he
tempted the Savior with the kingdoms of the

earth. The devil's attempt was no more false and far less hypocritical. But let me forbear, remembering it is also written, 'Judge not lest ye be judged.'"

TO THE COLORED PEOPLE OF BALTIMORE

To the colored people of Baltimore who presented him with a costly Bible on July 4th, 1864:

"In regard to the great book, I have only to say, it is the best gift which God has ever given man.

"All the good from the Savior of the World is communicated to us through this book. But for that book we could not know right from wrong. All those things desirable to man are contained in it. I return you my sincere thanks for this very elegant copy of the great book of God which you present."

TO THE EVANGELICAL LUTHERANS

"You well know, gentlemen, and the world knows, how reluctantly I accepted this issue of battle forced upon me on my advent to this place by the internal enemies of our country. You all know, the world knows, the forces and the resources the public agents have brought into employment to sustain a government against which there has been brought not one complaint of real injury committed against society at home

Mrs. Lincoln as Mistress of the White House

or abroad. You all may recollect that in taking up the sword thus forced into our hands, this government appealed to the prayers of the pious and the good, and declared that it placed its whole dependence upon the favor of God. I now humbly and reverently, in your presence, reiterate the acknowledgment of that dependence, not doubting that, if it shall please the Divine Being who determines the destinies of nations, this shall remain a united people, and that they will, humbly seeking the Divine guidance, make their prolonged national existence a source of new benefits to themselves and their successors, and to all classes and conditions of mankind."

TO A DELEGATION OF METHODISTS, MAY 14, 1864

"Nobly sustained as the government has been by all the churches, I would utter nothing which might in the least appear invidious against any. Yet without this it may fairly be said that the Methodist Episcopal Church, not less devoted than the best, is by its greater numbers the most important of all. It is no fault in others that the Methodist Church sends more soldiers to the field, more nurses to the hospital, and more prayers to Heaven than any. God bless the Methodist Church; bless all the churches and blessed be God, who, in this our great trial, giveth us the churches."

TO THE PRESBYTERIANS, MAY 30, 1863

"As a pilot I have used my best exertions to keep afloat our Ship of State, and shall be glad to resign my trust at the appointed time to another pilot more skilful and successful than I may prove. In every case and at all hazards the government must be perpetuated. Relying, as I do, upon the Almighty Power, and encouraged, as I am, by these resolutions which you have just read, with the support which I receive from Christian men, I shall not hesitate to use all the means at my control to secure the termination of this rebellion, and will hope for success."

TO ARCHBISHOP HUGHES, OCTOBER 21, 1861

"I find no law authorizing the appointment of chaplains for our hospitals; and yet the services of chaplains are more needed, perhaps, in the hospitals than with the healthy soldiers in the field. With this view, I have given a sort of quasi-appointment (a copy of which I enclose) to each of three Protestant ministers, who have accepted and entered upon the duties.

"If you perceive no objection, I will thank you to give me the name or names of one or more suitable persons of the Catholic Church, to whom I may with propriety tender the same service."

CAN'T GO TO HEAVEN

On Thursday of a certain week, two ladies,

from Tennessee, came before the President, asking the release of their husbands, held as prisoners of war at Johnson's Island. They were put off until Friday, when they came again, and were again put off until Saturday. At each of the interviews one of the ladies urged that her husband was a religious man. On Saturday, when the President ordered the release of the prisoner, he said to this lady:

"You say your husband is a religious man; tell him, when you meet him, that I say I am not much of a judge of religion, but that in my opinion the religion which sets men to rebel and fight against their government, because, as they think, that government does not sufficiently help some men to eat their bread in the sweat of other men's faces, is not the sort of religion upon which people can get to Heaven."

TO MRS. GURNEY, WIFE OF PASTOR OF THE CHURCH HE ATTENDED

"In the very responsible position in which I happen to be placed, being a humble instrument in the hands of our Heavenly Father as I am, and as we all are, to work out His great purposes, I have desired that all my works and acts may be according to His will, and that it might be so, I have sought His aid; but if, after endeavoring to do my best in the light which He affords me, I find my

efforts fail, I must believe that, for some purpose
unknown to me, He wills it otherwise. If I had
had my way, this war would never have been commenced. If I had been allowed my way, this war
would have been ended before this; but we find
it still continues, and we must believe that He
permits it for some wise purpose of His own,
mysterious and unknown to us; and though with
our limited undersiandings we may not be able to
comprehend it, yet we cannot but believe that He
who made the world still governs it."

TO MRS. E. P. GURNEY

"I am much indebted to the good Christian
people of the country for their constant prayers
and consolations; and to no one of them more
than to yourself. The purposes of the Almighty
are perfect, and must prevail, though we erring
mortals may fail to accurately perceive them in
advance. We hoped for a happy termination of
this terrible war long before this; but God knows
best, and has ruled otherwise. We shall yet ac-
knowledge His wisdom, and our own error
therein. Meanwhile we must work earnestly in
the best lights He gives us, trusting that so working still conduces to the great ends He ordains.
Surely He intends some great good to follow this
mighty convulsion, which no mortal could make,
and no mortal could stay."

READ THE BIBLE

A year before his death, addressing his friend Joshua Speed, he said:

"I am profitably engaged reading the Bible. Try to comprehend as much as possible of this book with your mind and accept the rest with faith, and you will live and die a better man."

GOD WILL NOT DESERT ME

Lincoln was greatly disturbed when the Secretary of the Treasury tendered his resignation. He named Senator Fessenden as his successor, but Fessenden declined the appointment. Lincoln, deeply moved, said to Fessenden:

"God has not deserted me as yet, and He will not desert me now."

EMANCIPATING THE SLAVES

A few days before issuing the Emancipation Proclamation he expressed himself to several of his cabinet members:

"I have made a solemn vow that as soon as Gen. Lee shall have been driven out of Pennsylvania, I will crown the event by emancipating the slaves."

SHOULD BE ON THE LORD'S SIDE

To the remark of a clergyman that he hoped "the Lord was on our side": "I am not concerned about that," replied Lincoln, "for I know that the Lord is always on the side of the right. But it is my constant anxiety and prayer that I and this Nation should be on the Lord's side."

.   .   .   .   .   .

"The purposes of the Almighty are perfect, and must prevail, though we erring mortals may fail to accurately perceive them in advance."

.   .   .   .   .   .

"God must like common people, or he would not have made so many of them."

SENDS MESSAGES VIA CHICAGO?

Characteristic is the reply Lincoln once gave a delegation of Chicago ministers, who had come to demand that he proclaim the liberty of states. The speaker of the delegates closed with these words: "This is a message from the Lord that is coming to you!"

"Ah," was Lincoln's sarcastic reply. "I did not know that the Lord sends me His messages by way of Chicago."

HIS LAST WORDS TO HIS WIFE

"There is no city in this world that I should like to see as much as Jerusalem."

These were Lincoln's last words addressed to his wife. He had hardly spoken them when the bullet of the murderer struck him down. (Emily Todd Helm in McClure's, September, 1898.)

One of the Most Interesting of all Lincoln Portraits

What a remarkable coincidence. When Lincoln said these words, he had in mind an earthly city, the Jerusalem of the Orient.

This desire was not fulfilled, but instead, he was to see the more beautiful, the holy city—the heavenly Jerusalem.

STATE PAPERS

FIRST INAUGURAL ADDRESS

"Why should there not be a patient confidence in the ultimate justice of the people? Is there any better or equal hope in the world? In our present differences is either party without faith of being in the right? If the Almighty Ruler of Nations, with His eternal truth and justice, be on your side of the North, or on yours of the South, that truth and that justice will surely prevail by the judgment of this great tribunal of the American people.

"If it were admitted that you who are dissatisfied hold the right side in the dispute, there still is no single good reason for precipitate action. Intelligence, patriotism, Christianity and a firm reliance on Him who has never yet forsaken this favored land, are still competent to adjust in the best way all our present difficulty.

"In your hands, my dissatisfied fellow-countrymen, and not in mine, is the momentous issue of civil war. The government will not assail you. You can have no conflict without being yourselves the aggressors. You have no oath registered in Heaven to destroy the government, while I shall have the most solemn one to 'preserve, protect and defend it.'"

EMANCIPATION PROCLAMATION

"And upon this act, sincerely believed to be an act of justice, warranted by the Constitution upon military necessity, I invoke the considerate judgment of mankind and the gracious favor of Almighty God."

SECOND INAUGURAL ADDRESS

"Neither party expected for the war the magnitude or the duration which it has already attained. Neither anticipated that the cause of the conflict might cease with, or even before, the conflict itself should cease. Each looked for an easier triumph, and a result less fundamental and astounding. Both read the same Bible, and pray to the same God; and each invokes His aid against the other. It may seem strange that any man should dare to ask a just God's assistance in wringing his bread from the sweat of other men's faces; but let us judge not, that we be not judged. The prayers of both could not be answered—that of neither has been answered fully.

"The Almighty has His own purposes. 'Woe unto the world because of offenses! for it must needs be that offenses come; but woe to that man by whom the offense cometh.' If we shall suppose that American slavery is one of those offenses which, in the providence of God, must needs come, but which, having continued through His appointed time, He now wills to remove, and that He gives to both North and South this terrible war as the woe due to those by whom the offense came, shall we discern therein any departure from

Lincoln and His Cabinet

those Divine attributes which the believers in a living God always ascribe to Him? Fondly do we hope, — fervently do we pray — that this mighty scourge of war may speedily pass away. Yet, if God wills that it continue until all the wealth piled by the bondman's two hundred and fifty years of unrequited toil shall be sunk, until every drop of blood drawn with the lash shall be paid by another drawn with the sword, as was said three thousand years ago, so still it must be said, 'The judgments of the Lord are true and righteous altogether.'

"With malice toward none; with charity for all; with firmness in the right, as God gives us to see the right, let us strive on to finish the work we are in; to bind up the nation's wounds; to care for him who shall have borne the battle, and for his widow, and his orphan—to do all which may achieve and cherish a just and lasting peace among ourselves, and with all nations."

GETTYSBURG ADDRESS, NOVEMBER 19, 1863

"But, in a larger sense, we cannot dedicate— we cannot consecrate—we cannot hallow—this ground. The brave men, living and dead, who struggled here, have consecrated it far above our poor power to add or detract. The world will little note nor long remember what we say here, but it can never forget what they did here. It is for us, the living, rather, to be dedicated here to the unfinished work which they who fought here have thus far so nobly advanced. It is rather for us to be here dedicated to the great task remaining before us—that from these honored dead we take increased devotion to that cause for which they gave the last full measure of devotion; that we here highly resolve that these dead shall not have died in vain; that this nation, under God, shall have a new birth of freedom; and that government of the people, by the people, for the people, shall not perish from the earth."

ORDER FOR SABBATH OBSERVANCE, NOVEMBER 15, 1862

"The President, commander-in-chief of the army and navy, desires and enjoins the orderly observance of the Sabbath by the officers and men in the military and naval service. The importance to man and beast of the prescribed weekly rest, the sacred rights of Christian soldiers and sailors, a becoming deference to the best sentiment of a Christian people, and a due regard for the Divine will, demand that Sunday labor in the army and navy be reduced to the measure of strict necessity. The discipline and character of the national forces should not suffer, nor the cause they defend be imperiled, by the profanation of the day or name of the Most High.

'At this time of public distress'—adopting the words of Washington in 1776—'men may find enough to do in the service of God and their country without abandoning themselves to vice and immorality.' The first general order issued by the Father of his Country after the Declaration of Independence indicates the spirit in which our institutions were founded and should ever be defended. 'The general hopes and trusts that every officer and man will endeavor to live and act as becomes a Christian soldier, defending the dearest rights and liberties of his country.'"

IN MESSAGE TO CONGRESS, JULY 1, 1861

"Having thus chosen our course, without guile and with pure purpose, let us renew our trust in God, and go forward without fear and with manly hearts."

IN A LETTER TO SECRETARY STANTON, FEBRUARY 11, 1864

"I have never interfered nor thought of interfering as to who shall or shall not preach in any church; nor have I knowingly or believingly tolerated any one else to so interfere by my authority. If any one is so interfering by color of my authority, I would like to have it specifically made known to me. . . . I will not have control of any church on any side." (Nicolay and Hay.)

TO GENERAL CURTIS, JANUARY, 1864

"The United States Government must not undertake to run the churches. When an individual in a church or out of it becomes dangerous to the public interest, he must be checked, but the churches must take care of themselves. It will not do for the United States Government to appoint agents for the churches."

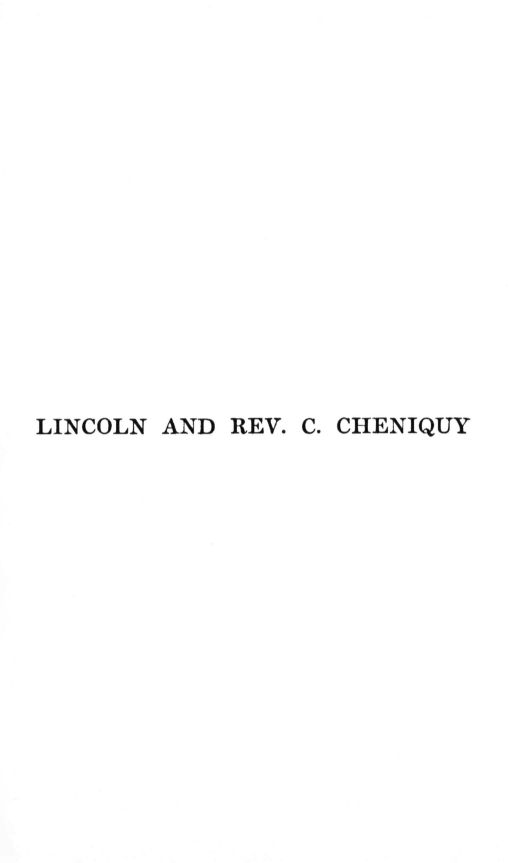

LINCOLN AND REV. C. CHENIQUY

In concluding we cannot deny ourselves the privilege of repeating the sublime words which the Rev. C. Cheniquy ascribes to Lincoln; words, the authenticity of which is doubted by some, although others are fully satisfied that they are genuine. While the words are here repeated without comment as to their reliability, it must be admitted that, when compared with what Lincoln said to Bateman, Gillespie and Gov. Bramlett, and when we place side by side with them the sublime words of Lincoln's second inaugural address and of other state papers, it does not appear impossible that these words of Lincoln are really authentic. They are so eloquent, so sublime, that one almost feels as if they were inspired, as such words seldom come from the lips of mortals.

Cheniquy believed that he had proof that Lincoln's assassination had been planned by some certain faction. He went to Washington to warn Lincoln to be on his guard. Lincoln, who had made Cheniquy's acquaintance in a law suit, in which he represented him, gave an audience to the former priest. After Cheniquy had explained his errand Lincoln replied in part:

"You are not the first to warn me against the dangers of assassination. My ambassadors in Italy, France and England, as well as Professor Morse, have, many times, warned me against the plots of the murderers whom they have detected in those different countries. But I see no other safeguard against those murderers, but to be always ready to die, as Christ advises it. As we must all die sooner or later, it makes very little difference to me whether I die from a dagger plunged through the heart or from an inflammation of the lungs. Let me tell you that I have, lately, read a message in the Old Testament which has made a profound, and, I hope, a salutary impression on me. Here is that passage."

The President took his Bible, opened it at the third chapter of Deuteronomy, and read from the 22nd to the 28th verse:

" '22· Ye shall not fear them; for the Lord your God shall fight for you.

" '23· And I besought the Lord at that time, saying:

" '24· O Lord God, thou hast begun to show thy servant thy greatness, and thy mighty hand; for what God is there, in heaven or in earth, that can do according to thy words, and according to thy might!

" '25· I pray thee, let me go over and see the good land that is beyond Jordan, that goodly mountain, and Lebanon.

" '26· But God was wroth with me for your sakes, and would not hear me: and the Lord said unto me, let it suffice thee: speak no more unto me of this matter:

Lincoln in 1864

" '27· Get thee up unto the top of Pisgah, and lift up thine eyes westward and northward, and southward and eastward, and behold it with thine eyes; for thou shalt not go over this Jordan.' "

After the President had read these words with great solemnity, he added:

"My dear Father Cheniquy, let me tell you that I have read these strange and beautiful words several times, these last five or six weeks. The more I read them, the more, it seems to me, that God has written them for me as well as for Moses.

"Has He not taken me from my poor log cabin, by the hand, as He did of Moses in the reeds of the Nile, to put me at the head of the greatest and most blessed of modern nations just as He put that prophet at the head of the most blessed nation of ancient times? Has not God granted me a privilege, which was not granted to any living man, when I broke the fetters of 4,000,000 of men, and made them free? Has not our God given me the most glorious victories over our enemies? Are not the armies of the Confederacy so reduced to a handful of men, when compared to what they were two years ago, that the day is fast approaching when they will have to surrender?

"Now, I see the end of this terrible conflict, with the same joy of Moses, when at the end of his trying forty years in the wilderness; and I pray my God to grant me to see the days of peace and

untold prosperity, which will follow this cruel
war, as Moses asked God to see the other side of
Jordan, and enter the Promised Land. But, do
you know, that I hear in my soul, as the voice of
God, giving me the rebuke which was given to
Moses?

"Yes! every time that my soul goes to God to
ask the favor of seeing the other side of Jordan,
and eating the fruits of that peace, after which I
am longing with such an unspeakable desire, do
you know that there is a still but solemn voice
which tells me that I will see those things only
from a long distance, and that I will be among
the dead when the nation, which God granted me
to lead through those awful trials, will cross the
Jordan, and dwell in that Land of Promise, where
peace, industry, happiness and liberty will make
every one happy; and why so? Because He has
already given me favors which He never gave, I
dare say, to any man in these latter days.

"Why did God Almighty refuse to Moses the
favor of crossing the Jordan, and entering the
Promised Land? It was on account of the nation's sins! That law of Divine retribution and
justice, by which one must suffer for another, is
surely a terrible mystery. But it is a fact which
no man who has any intelligence and knowledge
can deny. Moses, who knew that law, though he
probably did not understand it better than we do,
calmly says to his people: 'God was wroth with
me for your sakes.'

"But, though we do not understand that mysterious and terrible law, we find it written in letters of tears and blood wherever we go. We do not read a single page of history without finding undeniable traces of its existence.

"Where is the mother who has not shed tears and suffered real tortures, for her children's sake?

"Who is the good king, the worthy emperor, the gifted chieftain, who have not suffered unspeakable mental agonies, or even death, for their people's sake?

"Is not our Christian religion the highest expression of the wisdom, mercy and love of God! But what is Christianity if not the very incarnation of that eternal law of Divine justice in our humanity?

"When I look on Moses, alone, silently dying on the Mount Pisgah, I see that law, in one of its most sublime human manifestations, and I am filled with admiration and awe.

"But when I consider that law of justice, and expiation in the death of the Just, the divine Son of Mary, on the mountain of Calvary, I remain mute in my adoration. The spectacle of the Crucified One which is before my eyes is more than sublime, it is divine! Moses died for his people's sake, but Christ died for the whole world's sake! Both died to fulfill the same eternal law of the Divine justice, though in a different measure.

"Now, would it not be the greatest of honors

and privileges bestowed upon me, if God, in His infinite love, mercy and wisdom, would put me between His faithful servant, Moses, and His eternal Son, Jesus, that I might die as they did, for my nation's sake!

"My God alone knows what I have already suffered for my dear country's sake. But my fear is that the justice of God is not yet paid. When I look upon the rivers of tears and blood drawn by the lashes of the merciless masters from the veins of the very heart of those millions of defenseless slaves, these two hundred years; when I remember the agonies, the cries, the unspeakable tortures of those unfortunate people to which I have, to some extent, connived with so many others a part of my life, I fear that we are still far from the complete expiation. For the judgments of God are true and righteous.

"It seems to me that the Lord wants to-day, as He wanted in the days of Moses, another victim— a victim which He has Himself chosen, anointed and prepared for the sacrifice, by raising it above the rest of His people. I cannot conceal from you that my impression is that I am the victim. So many plots have already been made against my life, that it is a real miracle that they have all failed. But can we expect that God will make a perpetual miracle to save my life? I believe not.

"But just as the Lord heard no murmur from the lips of Moses, when He told him that he had to die before crossing the Jordan, for the sins of his people, so I hope and pray that He will hear no murmur from me when I fall for my nation's sake.

"The only two favors I ask of the Lord, are, first, that I may die for the sacred cause in which I am engaged, and when I am the standard-bearer of the rights and liberties of my country.

"The second favor I ask from God, is that my dear son, Robert, when I am gone, will be one of those who lift up that flag of Liberty which will cover my tomb, and carry it with honor and fidelity to the end of his life, as his father did, surrounded by the millions who will be called with him to fight and die for the defense and honor of our country."

"Never had I heard such sublime words," says Father Cheniquy. "Never had I seen a human face so solemn and so prophet-like as the face of the President, when uttering these things. Every sentence had come to me as a hymn from heaven, reverberated by the echoes of the mountains of Pisgah and Calvary. I was beside myself. Bathed in tears, I tried to say something, but I could not utter a word.

"I knew the hour to leave had come. I asked from the President permission to fall on my knees and pray with him that his life might be spared; and he knelt with me. But I prayed more with my tears and sobs than with my words.

"Then I pressed his hand on my lips and bathed it with my tears, and with a heart filled with an unspeakable desolation, I bade him Adieu! It was for the last time!

"For the hour was fast approaching when he was to fall by the hand of an assassin, for his nation's sake."

And with this we leave the reader to form his own opinion on the question: "Was Abraham Lincoln an infidel?"

The Last Portrait of **Abraham** Lincoln, Taken April 9, 1865,
the Sunday Before His Assassination

OPINIONS OF LINCOLN'S RELIGIOUS CHARACTER

HON. I. N. ARNOLD

"It is very strange that any reader of Lincoln's speeches and writings should have the hardihood to charge him with a want of religious feeling. No more reverent Christian than he ever sat in the Executive chair, not excepting Washington. . . . . From the time he left Springfield to his death he not only himself continually prayed for Divine assistance, but constantly asked the prayers of his friends for himself and his country. . . . . Doubtless, like many others, he passed through periods of doubt and perplexity. . . . . When the unbeliever shall convince the people that this man whose life was straightforward, clear and honest, was a sham and a hypocrite, then, but not before, may he make the world doubt his Christianity."

FRANCIS BICKNELL CARPENTER

"Doubtless Lincoln felt as deeply upon the great questions of the soul and eternity as any other thoughtful man; but the very tenderness and humility of his nature would not permit the exposure of his inmost convictions, except upon the rarest occasions, and to his most intimate friends. And yet, aside from emotional expression, I believe no man had a more abiding sense of his dependence upon God, or faith in the Divine government, and in the power and ultimate triumph of Truth and Right in the world."

J. G. HOLLAND

"Lincoln was a religious man. This fact may be stated without any reservation—with only an explanation. He believed in God, and in His personal supervision of the affairs of men. He believed himself to be under His control and guidance. He believed in the power and ultimate triumph of the right, through his belief in God. This unwavering faith in a Divine Providence began at his mother's knee, and ran like a thread of gold through all the inner experiences of his life. His constant sense of human duty was one of the forms by which his faith manifested itself. His conscience took a broader grasp than the simple apprehension of right and wrong. He recognized an immediate relation between God and himself, in all the actions and passions of his life. He was not professedly a Christian—that is, he subscribed to no creed—joined no organization of Christian disciples. He spoke little then, perhaps less than he did afterward, and always sparingly, of his religious belief and experiences; but that he had a deep religious life, sometimes imbued with superstition, there is no doubt. We guess at a mountain of marble by the outcropping ledges that hide their whiteness among the ferns."

Holland closes his remarks about Lincoln's character as follows: "Mr. Lincoln's character was one which will grow. It will become the basis of an ideal man. It was so pure, and so unselfish, and so rich in its materials, that fine imaginations will spring from it, to blossom and bear fruit through all the centuries. This element was found in Washington, whose human weaknesses seem to have faded entirely from memory, leaving him a demi-god; and it will be found in Mr. Lincoln in a still more remarkable degree. The black race have already crowned him. With the black man, and particularly the black freedman, Mr. Lincoln's name is the saintliest which he pronounces, and the noblest he can conceive. To the emancipated, he is more than man—a being scarcely second to the Lord Jesus Christ Himself. That old, white-headed negro who undertook to tell you what 'Massa Linkum' was to his dark-minded brethren, embodied the vague conceptions of his race in the words: 'Massa Linkum, he ebery whar; he know ebery ting; he walk de carf like de Lord.' He was to these men the incarnation of power and goodness; and his memory will live in the hearts of this unfortunate and oppressed race while it shall exist upon the earth."

HE WAS A VERY HUMBLE MAN

Another writer says:

"Certainly, Mr. Lincoln's religion was very different from this. It was one which sympathized with all human sorrow; which lifted, so far as it had the power, the burden from the oppressed; which let the prisoner go free, and which called daily for supplies of strength and wisdom from the divine fountains. He grew more religious with every passing year of his official life. The tender piety that breathed in some of his late state papers is unexampled in any of the utterances of his predecessors. In all the great emergencies of his closing years, his reliance upon Divine guidance and assistance was often extremely touching. 'I have been driven many times to my knees,' he once remarked, 'by the overwhelming conviction that I had nowhere else to go. My own wisdom and that of all about me seemed insufficient for that day.' On another occasion, when told that he was daily remembered in the prayers of those who prayed, he said that he had been a good deal helped by the thought; and then he added with much solemnity: 'I should be the most presumptuous blockhead upon this footstool, if I for one day thought that I could discharge the duties which have come upon me since I came into this place without the aid and enlightenment of One who is wiser and stronger than all others.' He always remained shy in the exposure of his religious experiences, but those around him caught golden glimpses of a beautiful Christian character. With failing strength and constant weariness, the even temper of the man sometimes gave way, while his frequent experience of the faithlessness and cupidity of men

Old Ford's Theatre, Where President Lincoln Was Shot

made him at last distrustful of those who approached him."

Nicolay and Hay, private secretaries to Lincoln, who certainly should have been able to form an unprejudiced judgment of Lincoln's character, have this to say:

"Lincoln was a man of profound and intense religious feeling. He continually invited and appreciated at their highest value the prayers of good people. From that morning when standing amid the falling snowflakes on the railway car at Springfield he asked the prayers of his neighbors in those touching phrases whose echo rose that night in invocations from thousands of family altars, to the memorable hour when, on the steps of the national capitol, he humbled himself before his Creator in the sublime words of the second inaugural, there is not an expression known to have come from his lips or his pen but proves that he held himself answerable in every act of his career to a more august tribunal than any on earth. The fact that he was not a communicant of any church and that he was singularly reserved in regard to his personal religious life gives only the greater force to these striking proofs of his profound reverence and faith."

JOHN G. NICOLAY

Outside of Lincoln's private family no one was more able to judge Lincoln's inner life than his private secretary, John G. Nicolay. He has this to say on the subject:

"I do not remember ever having discussed religion with Mr. Lincoln, nor do I know of any authorized statement of his views in existence. He sometimes talked freely, and never made any concealment of his belief or unbelief in any dogma or doctrine, but never provoked religious controversies. I speak more from his disposition and habits than from any positive declaration on his part. He frequently made remarks about sermons he had heard, books he had read, or doctrines that had been advanced, and my opinion as to his religious belief is based upon such casual evidence. There is not the slightest doubt that he believed in a Supreme Being of omnipotent power and omniscient watchfulness over the children of men, and that this Being could be reached by prayer.

"Mr. Lincoln was a praying man. I know that to be a fact. And I have heard him request people to pray for him, which he would not have done had he not believed that prayer is answered. . . . I have heard him say that he prayed for this or that, and remember one occasion on which he remarked that if a certain thing did not occur he would lose his faith in prayer. . . . At the same time he did not believe in some of the dogmas of the orthodox churches. He believed in the Bible, however. . . . He often declared that the Sermon on the Mount contained the essence of all law and justice, and the Lord's Prayer was the sublimest composition in human language."

SELECTIONS FROM LIST OF
The C. M. Clark Publishing Co.

WINDING WATERS. By Frances Parker.

Illustrated. Cloth. Price, $1.50.

Author of the two big Western successes: "Hope Hathaway" and "Marjie of the Lower Ranch." This is the first work from the pen of Miss Parker in four years. You will find in her new strong and compelling story of the Great West many startling disclosures of our land that will rouse criticism and interest.

TRACT NUMBER 3377. By George H. Higgins and Margaret Higgins Haffey.

Spendidly Illustrated. Cloth. Price, $1.50.

Tells how Ashton Walbridge, a young college man, enters the oil regions to make his fortune, and how he overcomes all obstacles You will admire Enoch, laugh at "Little Prue" and sympathize with Anna. Said by many critics who have read the advance sheets to be far and ahead of John Fox, Jr.'s "The Trail of the Lonesome Pine." Bound to be a big seller.

REAL LETTERS OF A REAL GIRL. By Betty.

Richly bound. Price, $1.25.

The author of this splendid book possesses that rarest of gifts, genuine and spontaneous humor. She has, moreover, the broad outlook of life and the people that travel in many lands, coupled with the keen observation and wit to record her impressions that makes her book at once unique and captivating.

THE HEART OF SILENCE. By Walter S. Cramp.

Richly bound. Price, $1.50.

The scene of the opening part of this story is laid in Italy with an American family, consisting of a retired manufacturer from the United States, his wife and daughter, who is the heroine, and a foster son. Around this family is woven a charming tale of love and romance. Not a dull line.

MY SOLDIER LADY. By Ella Hamilton Durley.

Illustrated. Cloth. Price, $1.25.

This bright little book gives the other half of the correspondence comprising that charming story, "The Lady of the Decoration," but is complete in itself and entirely independent and original in conception and heart interest. Five editions and still selling.

THE BELL COW. By Bryant E. Sherman.
Illustrated. Cloth. Price, $1.50.

Decidedly a story of simple country life. The trials and pleasures are those of the out-of-the-way places. There is plot strong enough to keep the reader's interest from cover to cover. Humor, pathos and excitement are all here, bnt the most important part is played by the Aunt Betsy, the old maid with the big heart.

ALICE BRENTON. By Mary Josephine Gale.
Illustrated. Cloth. Price, $1.50.

The author has drawn a vivid picture of Colonial Newport, with her wealth and culture, spacious mansions and handsome grounds.

Mrs. Gale describes the sufferings and privations of the people during those trying days, calls attention to the depredations of the soldiers, and in the end makes love triumph over all obstacles. The book has ingenuity in plot, and much interesting material.
—*The News, Newport, R. I.*

THE DOOR WHERE THE WRONG LAY. By Mary E. Greene.
Illustrated. Cloth. Price, $1.50.

A story that will well repay the reading is "The Door Where The Wrong Lay." The plot is a strange and unusual one, and the story is one which will linger in the memory long after many a lighter tale is forgotten.—*Boston Times.*

A KNIGHT IN HOMESPUN. By John Charles Spoth.
Illustrated. Cloth. Price, $1.50.

A homely little tale of wholesome sentiment, bearing the title, "A Knight In Homespun," has its scene mainly in and about Pocono Mountains in Eastern Pennsylvania. It is told through the medium of the old clock, which for many years had ticked off the time in the hall of the home of Dr. Henry Boosch, while it watched the development of the human drama which went on in the household.—*New York Times.*

UNCLE SIM. By Fred Perrine Lake.
Illustrated. Cloth. Price, $1.50.

A story with a charming rural setting is "Uncle Sim." It gives admirable portraiture of the types to be found in a country village—pleasant, kindly, royal-hearted folk, whose aquaintance is well worth the reader's while—*Boston Times.*

AT THE SIGN OF THE BLUE ANCHOR. By Grace R. Osgood.
Illustrated. Cloth. Price, $1.50.

This tale of Colonial Days in New Jersey takes one among charming people, through delightful and romantic scenes both in the Old World and New.

THE TOBACCO TILLER. By Sarah Bell Hackley.
Illustrated. Cloth. Price, $1.50.

A strong and compelling romance woven about an industry and placed in a section of the country that is attracting international attention at the present time.

IN THE TWILIGHT ZONE. By Roger Carey Craven.
Illustrated. Cloth. Price, $1.50.

A story of the South. It is instinct with ambitions, passions and problems of its strongly drawn characters.

THE DRAGNET. By Elizabeth B. Bohan.
Illustrated. Cloth. Price, $1.50.

A timely story dealing with the liquor question and municipal reform. These topics are interwoven in a powerful story, in a fearless way that will stimulate thought along these lines.

CHANEY'S STRATAGEM. By Hannah Courtenay Pinnix.
Illustrated. Cloth. Price, $1.50.

A striking piece of fiction. The sudden and unexpected turn of Fortune's Wheel, by which the heroine and the other characters find their level, makes mighty interesting reading.

TOMPKINSVILLE FOLKS. By Nettie Stevens.
Illustrated. Cloth. Price, $1.50.

Is a careful study of human nature in human life. The pathos and charm of its rural setting and homely characters are drawn with firm yet skilful touch.

THE CAREER OF JOY. By Grace Eleanore Towndrow.
Illustrated. Cloth. Price, $1.25.

Genuinely, tenderly, and with a pervasive charm impossible to describe, the author tells the story of the old love, which returns to the woman's life after the fetters of a loveless marriage enchain her. Which path shall she choose?

THE VASSALAGE. By Adelaide Fuller Bell.
Illustrated. Cloth. Price, $1.50.

The story is vivid, dramatic, picturesque, and the strong strange psychic forces in the lives of the principal characters add a wholly unique interest to the tale.

THE GARDEN SERIES

By CARRO FRANCES WARREN

WHEN completed will comprise SIX of the most fascinating, and at the same time uplifting and instructive stories for children ever written. The titles are:

(1) LITTLE BETTY MARIGOLD AND HER FRIENDS.
(2) LITTLE POLLY PRIMROSE AND HER FRIENDS.
(3) LITTLE GOLDIE GOLDENROD AND HER FRIENDS.
(4) LITTLE TOPSY THISTLE AND HER FRIENDS.
(5) LITTLE PETER PANSY.
(6) LITTLE DANNY DANDELION.

Of these the first two have already been issued, and numbers 3 and 4 will be published in 1909.

Each volume will contain a page showing all the flowers mentioned in the story, in all the beauty of their natural colors. These Nature studies will be of great interest and value to every child reader.

The many colored illustrations and handsome binding will make any or all of these volumes most attractive gift books for children. They will be sold at a uniform price of **75 cents each.**

At all Booksellers, or sent postpaid by

THE C. M. CLARK PUBLISHING CO.

211 Tremont Street, Boston, Massachusetts

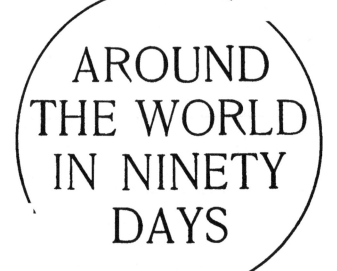

Made in the USA
Las Vegas, NV
13 February 2022

43802999R00092